D1759547

LUFTWAFFE UNIFORMS

J. P. Chantrain, R. Pied
and R. Smeets

Front cover illustration: Major Oesau with his Me 109. Note the tally on his tail, the Werke-Nummer (1559) and the yellow rudder. He is wearing a good quality animal skin fur-lined jacket with large collar, leather gloves, blue-grey tunic, officer's peaked cap with silver embroidered insignia and chincords, and the Knight's Cross.

Back cover illustration: Two great aces, Oberst (colonel) Galland (left) and Oberst Mölders. Galland wears a top-quality leather greatcoat with brown leather belt and holster, and Mölders displays his numerous orders and badges on his four-buttoned tunic, including the Spanish Cross with Swords (right breast), Iron Cross 1st Class, Pilot's Badge and Wounded Badge in black (left breast), ribbon of Iron Cross 2nd Class (buttonhole) and rank badges (shoulder-boards and collar patches). Both are wearing the Knight's Cross with Oakleaves and Swords, the highest German decoration for valour when this picture was taken.

1. Pilot and observer, with canvas flying helmets and rigid-framed shatterproof goggles with red lenses. The observer is manipulating the aircraft's camera switch, over an enemy AA site.

▼**1**

LUFTWAFFE UNIFORMS

J. P. Chantrain, R. Pied and R. Smeets

ARMS AND
ARMOUR

▲2 ▼3   ▼4

INTRODUCTION

First published in Great Britain in
1989 by Arms and Armour Press,
Artillery House, Artillery Row,
London SW1P 1RT.

Distributed in the USA by Sterling
Publishing Co. Inc., 387 Park
Avenue South, New York, NY
10016-8810, USA.

Distributed in Australia by
Capricorn Link (Australia) Pty. Ltd.,
P.O. Box 665, Lane Cove, New
South Wales 2066, Australia.

British Library Cataloguing in
Publication Data:
Chantrain, J. P.
Luftwaffe Uniforms. − (soldiers
fotofax)
1. Germany. Luftwaffe. Uniforms,
history
I. Title II. Pied, R. III. Smeets, Rene
IV. Series
358.4'11'40943
ISBN 1-85409-028-3

Designed and edited by DAG
Publications Ltd. Designed by
David Gibbons; layout by Cilla
Eurich; typeset by Ronset
Typesetters Ltd, Darwen
Lancashire, and by Typesetters
(Birmingham) Limited, Warley,
West Midlands; camerawork by
M&E Reproductions, North
Fambridge, Essex; printed and
bound in Great Britain by The
Alden Press Limited, Oxford.

U nder the terms of the Treaty of Versailles imposed by the victorious Allies in June 1919, Germany was forbidden to have a military air force. Furthermore, all aeronautical material extant – some 15,000 aeroplanes and 25,000 engines – was to be surrendered by 1920. However, Germany continued to produce civilian aircraft, many of which had potential for military use, and in 1926 the civil aeronautical company Lufthansa was established. This, together with ostensibly sporting associations such as the Deutsche LuftsportsVerband (DLV), which encouraged gliding activity, screened a great many ex-military pilots and observers for flying roles. And it was not long before military air crew were receiving secret training in the USSR. Germany's new air force was beginning to take shape.

The rise and fall of the Luftwaffe is encapsulated in the section beginning on page 24. In this pictorial study, we have concentrated our attention upon flying suits and gear. The centre section illustrates most of the service and dress uniforms with drawings taken from a 1938 book published for military tailors.

All pictures are from the collections of Jean-Pierre Chantrain and Robert Pied; the text and captions are by Rene Smeets. Insignia and uniform drawings are taken from the very rare 1938 edition of *Uniform Massschneidern für die Wehrmacht*, Fritz Hiddeman, Verlag Teubner, Leipzig/Berlin.

5 ▼

2. A group of NCOs from a dive-bombing unit. Note the fur-lined flying jackets, ski caps and the decorations worn on the flying blouse, including the German Cross in Gold (right breast) and the operational flying clasp (left breast).

3. A fighter pilot with the lightweight (net) version of the flying helmet (often called summer helmet). The large metal press-stud is intended to fix the oxygen mask.

4. A mechanic at work, wearing the special combination working suit.

5. An observer with canvas flying helmet and the shatterproof flying goggles; note the hook for the oxygen-mask, the binoculars and the aerial map.

▲6 ▶   ▲7   8▼   9▶

6. A pilot in a canvas flying suit, with its distinctive half yoke over the right shoulder, and trousers pockets, talking with a mechanic wearing a two-piece working rig; note other ranks' belt and buckle.

7. The scarf was traditional among flying personnel; note the details of the flying suit.

8. Observer at work. Note the details of the canvas flying helmet strap and buckle, and the leather protection of the earphone.

9. The last cigarette before the mission; note excellent detail of both canvas flying suit and helmet, and the special case for documents.

▲10

▲11

◀12

10. The camera, with its magazine full of exposed film, is taken from an observation aircraft.

11. The crew of an observation aircraft in the last moments before the mission, strapping on their parachutes. The man in the centre is clearly wearing a life-jacket (note the tube for inflation). Three different types of headgear are in use; the man on the right is evidently the observer with his binoculars and document case.

12. Waiting in the summer for comrades: the man on the left is not part of the aircrew (no qualification badge); an Obergefreiter, he wears the flying blouse with rank insignia and black Wounded Badge; (all insignia except collar patches were worn on the Luftwaffe shirt – breast eagle, shoulder straps, Iron Cross 1st Class). In the background, an officer pilot (note the cloth version of Pilot's Badge on left breast under the Iron Cross 1st Class).

13. Grand Admiral Doenitz visiting the Atlantic Coast. Note the mixing of uniform items, including tropical shirts, shorts and side cap (fourth man from the right, first row), grey-blue shirt and side cap (fifth from the right), grey-blue other ranks' flying blouse on tropical trousers (third from the right), with interesting insignia including the Wireless Operator/Air Gunner Badge), and black working suit (second from the right, with special NCO's collar braid).

14. The three men in the foreground are officers (denoted by rank insignia and silver piping on the side cap). Note the man in the centre wearing the kapok version of the life-jacket, most often used by bomber crews, and the man on the left wearing the Golden Badge of the Hitler Youth (diamond shaped) over one of several Nazi Rally Badges upgraded as official decorations.

▲15 ▼16

▲17

15. The officer on the left is wearing typical Luftwaffe breeches; the NCO wears the Wireless Operator/Air Gunner Badge and an Operational Flying Clasp.

16. All those officers in full dress, with steel helmet and the Flyer's Sword, are veterans of the First World War. The three on the right were flying personnel, as indicated by their First World War Flying Badges, with the Imperial Crown.

17. Classical walking-out dress for this Unteroffizier; note the rank badges on the collar patches and shoulder-straps, and the other ranks' quality peak cap with leather chinstrap and metal insignia.

18. One officer (note his officer's peaked cap) and many NCOs (no piping on their side caps) receiving instructions from their commanding officer. Note the details of the inflatable life-jacket.

19. The two models of life-jacket being worn concurrently; note the characteristic 'Channel' trousers, with their numerous pockets, worn over the flying boots by the man on the right, and inside the boots by the man on the left.

▲20 ▼21

22 ▲   23 ▶

20. The tally on the tail of a bomber, showing its ship victims. The difference between the officers' and other ranks' flying blouse and side cap is clearly visible.

21. Bomber crews, with the canvas flying suit and kapok life-jackets; the commanding officer, on the left, is wearing the peaked cap with the removable white top for summer wear.

22. A fighter pilot beside one of his victims early in the war. He is wearing an inflatable life-jacket, and the unit's cuffband on his right arm (here for the Jagdgeschwader Schlageter).

23. NCO in full dress with the Flyer's Sword; note the SA Sports Insignia and the specialist insignia for flying personnel not entitled to one of the Flying Badges (left cuff).

24. Flying gear for high-altitude flying, with electrical heating and oxygen mask.

▲25 ▼26 ▲27

25. Pre-war quality for this NCO's tunic, with the branch colour piping of the collar (discontinued during the war) and the first type of breast eagle (down-tailed). Note also the marksman's lanyard, the National Sports Badge and the NSFK gliding badge.

26. Three men from one of the Luftwaffe field divisions. Note the characteristic camouflaged jackets with Luftwaffe eagle and shoulder-straps.

27. Typical mixing of blue-grey uniforms and flying suits being worn concurrently by this bomber crew.

28. A scene at the operational school for wireless operators; note the details of the canvas flying helmet.

29. Note the different uniforms used by the recipients at this awarding ceremony. The large white stripes are clearly visible on the Field Marshal's trousers, on the left.

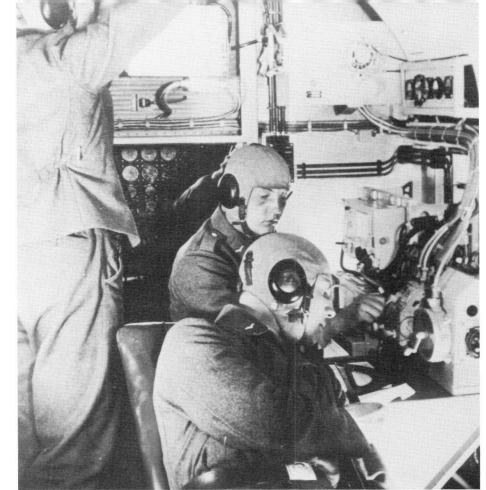

28 ▲   29 ▼

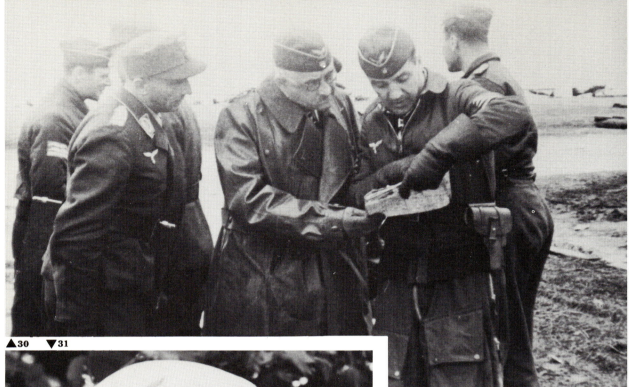

▲30 ▼31

30. A waterproof raincoat is worn by the officer in the centre of this picture. The man on the right is wearing multiple-pocket 'Channel' trousers with a leather flying jacket. Note the pistol case, and the special rank insignia for flying suit, worn by the Oberleutnant on the left.

31. This major is a veteran of the First World War (see his Pilot's Badge and First World War Iron Cross 1st Class). He is wearing a flying blouse of pre-war quality with an early down-tail breast eagle and DLV-type cap with removable white top. Note the place for a long ribbon bar.

32. Detail of the internal side of the kapok life-jacket; note also the double straps/buckles system of the canvas flying helmet.

33. Briefing: note the fur flying suit with typical zips, and the special rank insignia on both upper arms for Oberleutnant at left (one bar and two wings) and for Feldwebel (three wings) at right.

◀34 ▲35

34. Side and rear view of the special black working rig for mechanics.

35. The special box for signal pistol ammunition; note the different colour bars for different types of flares.

36. Three different types of flying helmets; the one on the left is leather.

37. Tropical shirt, side cap and trousers, all tan in colour; the trousers with large map pocket were also used by paratroopers.

36 ▼   37 ▶

38. A trainee during a flight: note the large goggles with rubber frames.

39. A Luftwaffe war correspondent (Kriegsberichter) in action.

40. Champagne for the hundredth mission; this kind of unofficial ceremony was very popular amongst flyers.

41. Some of the survival equipment carried aboard each aircraft.

▲38 ▼39

RANK INSIGNIA

The background and piping of the other ranks' collar patches and shoulder-straps, and the underlay of the officers' shoulder-boards insignia illustrated here were coloured according to branch of service. However, the colour for generals was white, the design embroidered in gold, with gold piping. Officers' collar patches were embroidered and piped in silver.

1–10: Other ranks' insignia. Those wearing insignia 3–8 also wore, respectively, one, two and three silver chevrons on the left upper arm.
1, 2: Flieger (or Kanonier, Funker, etc., depending on the branch of service).
3, 4: Gefreiter.

5, 6: Obergefreiter.
7, 8: Hauptgefreiter.
9, 10: The silver bar of a ribbon, here for Flieger, denoted an NCO candidate.

11–22: Non commissioned officers' rank insignia. Numbers 13, 16, 19 and 22 depict the collar patches for the greatcoat; the NCOs' tunic had a silver ribbon around the collar rather than on the patches themselves.
11, 12, 13: Unteroffizier
14, 15, 16: Unterfeldwebel
17, 18, 19: Feldwebel
20, 21, 22: Oberfeldwebel.

23–34: Officers' rank insignia
23, 24: Leutnant
25, 26: Oberleutnant

27, 28: Hauptmann
29, 30: Major
31, 32: Oberstleutnant
33, 34: Oberst.

35–42: General officers' rank insignia
35, 36: Generalmajor
37, 38: Generalleutnant
39, 40: General der Flieger (or der Flakartillerie, etc., depending upon branch of service).
41, 42: Genraloberst.
The ranks of Generalfeldmarschall (all gold shoulder-boards with silver crossed batons, same collar patches as 42, with silver crossed batons under the swastika) and of Reichsmarschall (unique rank awarded only to Goering, with successive special insignia) are not illustrated.

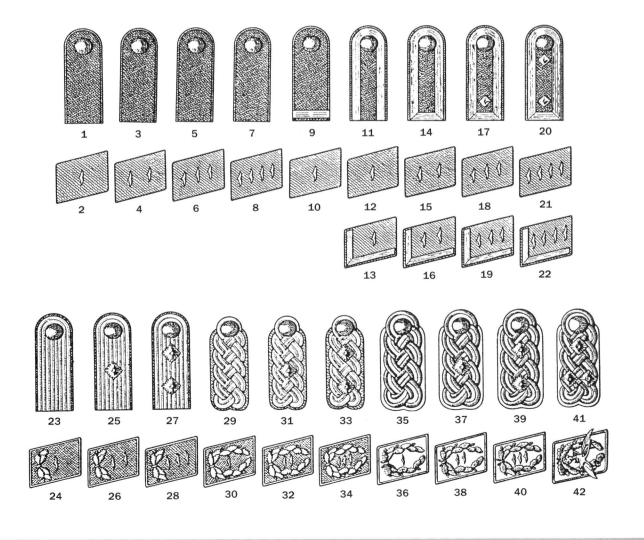

AIRCREW AND QUALIFICATION BADGES

This table shows but a selection of the aircrew badges awarded after qualification as pilot, observer, radio operator, etc., and of the trade insignia. The latter were worn exclusively by other ranks and NCOs.

1–4 show flying badges worn on the left pocket.

1: Pilots' badge introduced in March 1936; silver wreath, black eagle. (The same design with gilt wreath and silver eagle denoted the combined pilot/observer badge.)

2: Observers' badge introduced in 1936; wreath silver, eagle in black.

3: Aircrew badge introduced in January 1935 and discarded in March 1936; silver wreath and swastika, black eagle.

4: Air gunner/wireless operators' badge introduced in March 1936; silver wreath, black eagle. (The same design without the flashes in eagle's claws, introduced in June 1942, was the air gunner/flight engineers' badge.)

5–25: Speciality and qualification badges worn on the left sleeve above the cuff

5: Aircrew not entitled to one of the other aircrew badges

6: Flying technical personnel.

7: Administrative NCO.

8: Mechanized equipment administrator.

9: Aircraft equipment administrator.

10: Searchlight equipment administrator.

11: Signals equipment administrator.

12: Qualified telephonist.

13: NCO qualified telephonist.

14: Qualified telegraphist.

15: NCO qualified telegraphist.

16: Qualified radio operator.

17: NCO qualified radio operator.

18: Signals personnel for aircrew and Flak branches.

19: Ordnance personnel.

20: NCO armourer (aircrew and signals branches).

21: NCO armourer (Flak and Hermann Goering branches).

22: Medical personnel.

23: Motor vehicle driver.

24: Flak artillery personnel with 9 months' service.

25: Standard bearer; worn on upper right arm; the colour of the embroidered flags depended upon the branch of service.

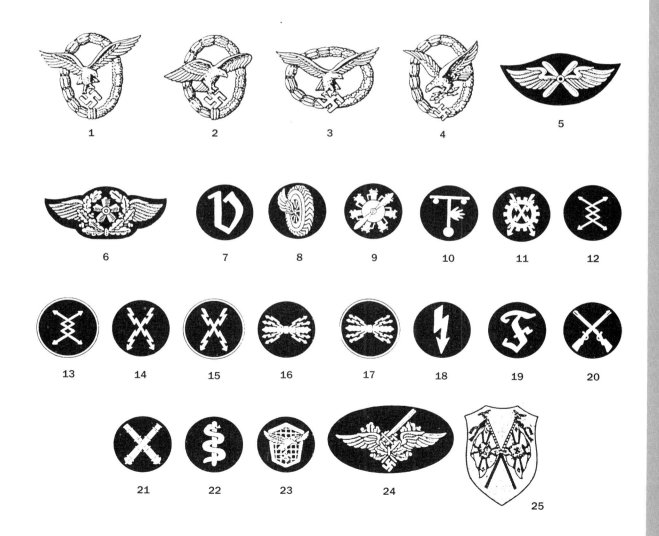

CHRONICLE OF THE LUFTWAFFE

After Hitler came to power in 1933, two of his closest associates were experienced airmen: Goering and Milch were placed respectively as Air Minister and Head of Lufthansa. In March 1935 the new Air Force or Luftwaffe was officially activated with Goering as Commander-in-Chief and Milch as Secretary of State. It immediately took charge of some 2,000 aircraft of varying types as well as 20,000 men, and 30 or 40 companies now began work designing and manufacturing engines and airframes in order to meet the first military production schedule, which called for 300 aircraft per month. Nazi flying organizations flourished: a Hitler Youth branch was formed, and the National Socialist Flying Corps absorbed the DLV.

Expansion of the Luftwaffe

By 1936 a number of new designs were in pre-production, among them the first types of Me 109 single-engined fighter,

Me 110 twin-engined fighter, Ju 87 dive-bomber and Ju 88, Do 17 and He 111 twin-engined and torpedo bombers. Soon a new arm, the Paratroopers, was formed within the Luftwaffe, in addition to the aircrews, ground crews and technical personnel. All these recruits wore the yellow branch colour (collar tabs, other ranks' shoulder-strap piping: officers' shoulder-board underlay and other ranks' peaked cap, piping). A very strong anti-aircraft artillery branch (bright red colouring) and sophisticated signals branch (brown colouring) were founded too.

Spain: Experience for War

In August 1936 the Spanish Civil War began. The Germans quickly organized an aerial force, the Condor Legion, which, clad in Spanish uniforms, went to the aid of Franco's Nationalists. The war was a splendid opportunity, fully exploited as such, during which to gain vital practical experience with their new fighters and bombers. The lessons offered by the war led the Luftwaffe to give precedence to dive-bombers and close-support aircraft at the expense of heavy bombers, a decision that left

1: Other ranks' and NCOs' walking-out dress with greatcoat (left) and pre-war four-buttoned tunic and trousers (right).

2: Officers' walking-out dress with four-buttoned tunic, breeches and boots.

Germany with an inability to respond to the Allied bombing campaigns later in the war.

Luftwaffe Organization

From September 1935 onwards, Germany was organized into four aerial regions, each with its own Air Fleet or Luftflotte. The four initial Luftflotten were eventually expanded to six, each combining an administrative regional division (Luftgau) and an operational division (Fliegerdivision, later renamed Flieger-korps). Naturally, the Luftwaffe was not restricted to flying; it also had Flak and Signals units, its own Medical Corps (dark blue branch colour), Construction Engineers (black branch colour), Military Administration (dark green branch colour with triangles instead of wings on the collar patches and double coloured underlay to the shoulder-boards), not to speak of many lesser known specialists such as the Music Corps and the Flying Engineers, with their pink branch colour (and propellers instead of wings on the collar tabs). Another ground unit, and an élite one, was the so-called 'Hermann Goering' Regiment (white branch colour), which developed over the years from a simple Police Regiment (Goering was once Minister President and Minister of Interior of Prussia) up to an Armoured-Paratroop Corps.

Luftwaffe at War

Needless to say, the Luftwaffe took a leading role in all the military actions between 1 September 1939 and 8 May 1945. The beginnings were spectacular, with the surprisingly swift success of the *Blitzkrieg* and easy victories in Poland and the Western campaign of May to June 1940. The first failure was the inability to wipe out the RAF during the Battle of Britain; then the Luftwaffe was heavily involved in the Battle for the Atlantic and the convoys running in the Mediterranean area: North Africa, the Balkans, Crete and Malta. Crete was the turning-point for the German paratroopers: they suffered very heavy losses and were never again dropped en masse, being used mainly as infantry thereafter. Malta was a disappointment too, the coordinated efforts of the Luftwaffe and the Italian Regia

3: Officers' flying blouse worn with breeches and boots.

4: Officers' white summer uniform.

5: Officers' greatcoat.

Aeronautica failing to crush the resistance of the heroic little island.

In June 1941 came the gigantic Eastern campaign. Once again the Luftwaffe was, with the armoured units, one of the main 'trump-cards' of the German High Command. At the end of the year, the new Fw 190 fighter began its operational career, deploying successfully against the under-powered Russian aircraft. The situation changed with the failure to reach Moscow before the formidable Russian winter set in, and 1942 saw the turn in Germany's fortunes. Allied landings in North Africa followed the victory of Montgomery at El Alamein; and the turning-point on the Eastern Front came at Stalingrad, with the loss of 600,000 men — partly because of the Luftwaffe's total inability to supply ammunition, food, spare parts, etc. to the encircled Sixth Army.

From the beginning of 1942, the Flak component of the Luftwaffe was regularly and rapidly expanded, growing to more than one million men. In 1943, with the expansion of Allied heavy bombing of German territory, substitute solutions were envisaged, with the drafting of about 75,000 members of the Hitler Youth as auxiliaries (Flakhelfer) to man searchlights and even the guns, alongside the 15,000 women (Flakhelferinnen) and men from the compulsory Labour Service (RAD) and even some Russian prisoners. The Civil Air Protection (Luftschutz), in existence before the war, was greatly expanded, and nearly all civilians became involved in one way or another in working with some Luftwaffe auxiliary organizations, such as the Warning Service (LSD) or the Security and Helping Service (SHD). More and more women were drafted for non-combatant roles, especially the operation of telephone and signals apparatus. In October 1942 the Luftwaffe Field Divisions were organized with men taken from ground crews, administrative units and Flak. Early in 1943 some 200,000 men were enlisted in these new infantry divisions, and they grew to the grand total of 22 divisions (wearing the new branch colour of rifle green).

The Defeat of the Luftwaffe
German industry, under the supervision of Minister Dr Todt and

6: Officers' informal evening dress (no stripes on trouser legs, blue waistcoat, black tie, ribbon bar).

7: Officers' formal evening dress (silver stripes on trouser legs, white waistcoat, white tie, medal bar).

8: Generals' special tunic with white lapels.

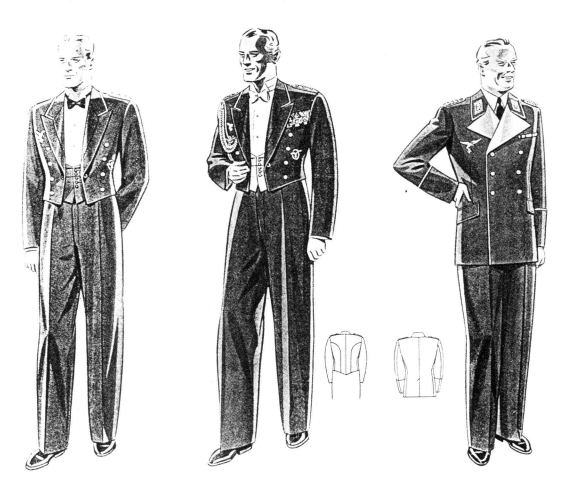

his successor Albert Speer, continued to expand its production during the war, with 1,000 fighters produced every month in June 1943; but this production could not compensate for the great losses increasingly incurred by inexperienced new pilots and aircrew. More and more of the aces were killed or shot down to become prisoners of war. The Reich's Defences, with more anti-aircraft units as well as day and night-fighters, tried to stop the Allied bombers, but they were unsuccessful. The introduction of new tactics, new weapons (air-to-air missiles, etc.) and jet aircraft (fighters like the Me 262, Me 163 and He 162 plus bombers like the Ar 264) were too little too late. The desperate attempt to break the spirit of the Allies through secret weapons like the V-1 pilotless flying bomb and the V-2 rocket also failed, and the Luftwaffe was gradually downgraded in the last months of the war, having halted neither the Red Army advance in the East nor the Allied armies in Italy and France.

By January 1945, only 1,875 operational aircraft were airworthy, among them 360 single-engined fighters, 100 twin-engined fighters, 270 night-fighters and only 80 bombers. The last brilliant, but doomed, action was the massive attack on Allied airfields on New Year's Eve 1945.

BIBLIOGRAPHY

The Rise and Fall of the German Air Force 1933–1945, Arms and Armour Press, London, 1987, reprinted from an official publication; excellent general history of the Luftwaffe, highly recommended.

The Luftwaffe by Roger James Bender, Bender Publishing, USA, 1972; currently the one and only book dealing with all uniforms and insignia of the Luftwaffe and its numerous related organizations, both military and political.

Fliegersonderbekleidung-und Ausrustung by H. D. Kraft, Uniform-und Ausrustung Deutscher Streitkrafte, Volume I, Patzwall, 1987; the first in a new series published in Germany, dealing with German flying suits and equipment.

9: Officers' cape.

10: Later model five-buttoned tunic that could be worn with collar open or closed.

LUFTWAFFE ORGANIZATION (SIMPLIFIED)

* Usually 90 aircraft. ** Usually 30 aircraft.
*** Usually 9–10 aircraft.

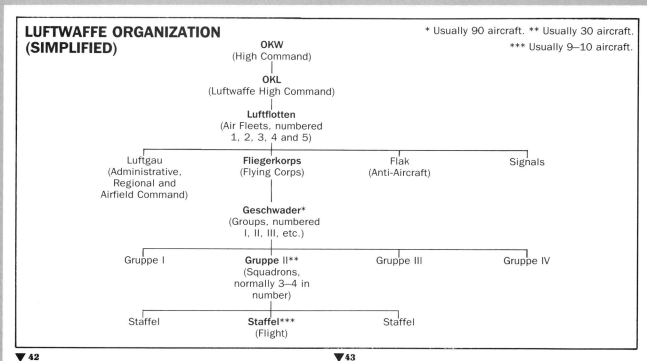

OKW
(High Command)

OKL
(Luftwaffe High Command)

Luftflotten
(Air Fleets, numbered
1, 2, 3, 4 and 5)

Luftgau
(Administrative,
Regional and
Airfield Command)

Fliegerkorps
(Flying Corps)

Flak
(Anti-Aircraft)

Signals

Geschwader*
(Groups, numbered
I, II, III, etc.)

Gruppe I

Gruppe II**
(Squadrons,
normally 3–4 in
number)

Gruppe III

Gruppe IV

Staffel

Staffel*
(Flight)

Staffel

▼ 42

▼ 43

44 ▲   45 ▼

46 ▲

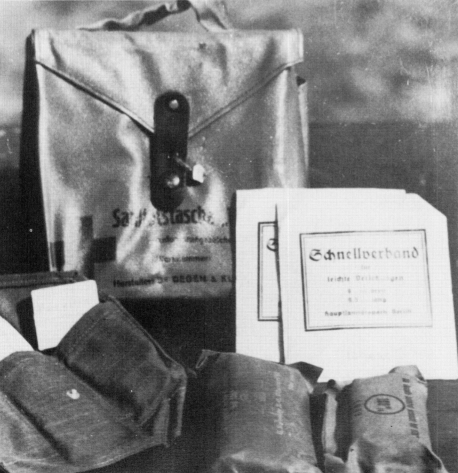

42. Another very good view of the special black working suit. Despite regulations, the black linen work cap was seldom worn with these work overalls.

43. This is the big 'special bag' (sealed) which held all the survival material illustrated by some of pictures here. The parachute rigger NCO was always in charge of the bag both before and during the flight.

44. The survival bag also contained two emergency ration containers; each held enough to feed one man for four days.

45. Another necessity in the survival bag was the medical material.

46. A useful item was the shovel/entrenching tool.

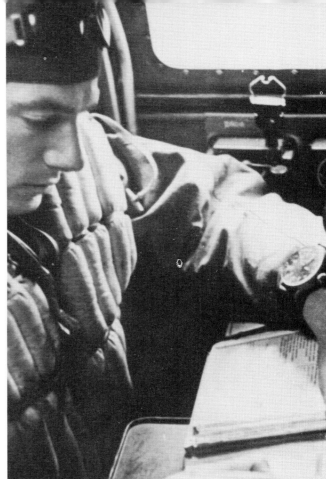

▲47 ▼48   ▲49

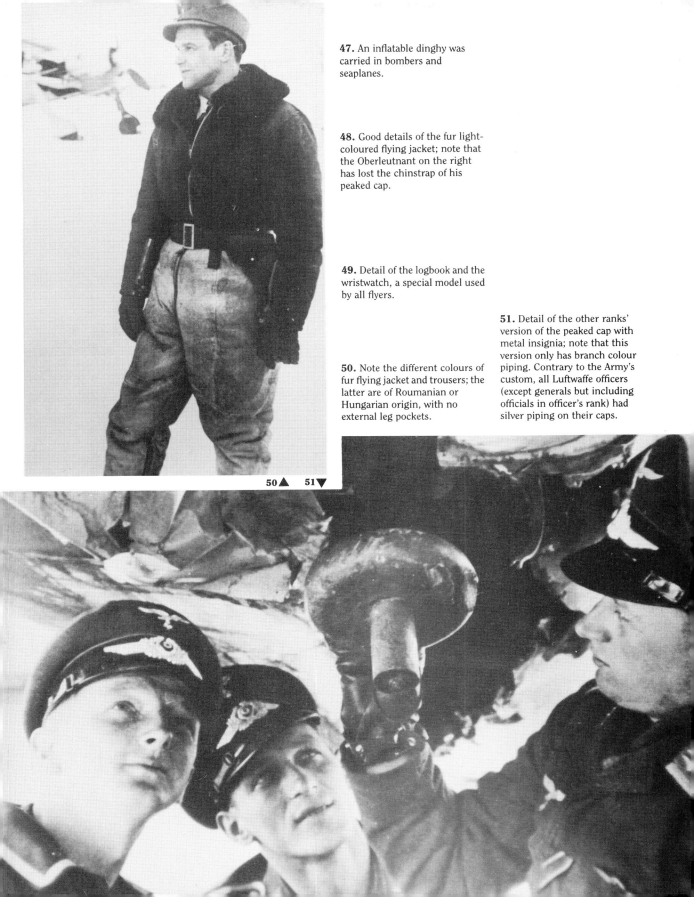

47. An inflatable dinghy was carried in bombers and seaplanes.

48. Good details of the fur light-coloured flying jacket; note that the Oberleutnant on the right has lost the chinstrap of his peaked cap.

49. Detail of the logbook and the wristwatch, a special model used by all flyers.

50. Note the different colours of fur flying jacket and trousers; the latter are of Roumanian or Hungarian origin, with no external leg pockets.

51. Detail of the other ranks' version of the peaked cap with metal insignia; note that this version only has branch colour piping. Contrary to the Army's custom, all Luftwaffe officers (except generals but including officials in officer's rank) had silver piping on their caps.

50▲   51▼

52. Bomber's machine-gunner. At the beginning of the war, they often wore steel helmets.

53. A good illustration of the leather greatcoat on the left, the standard officer's greatcoat in the centre, and the summer canvas flying suit on the right. The arm rank insignia seen here is for an Oberfeldwebel.

54. A propaganda picture showing the good mood of members of a unit that has completed 1000 sorties over England. Note the details of the summer flying suits, and the arm rank insignia for Unteroffizier (one wing).

55. Installation of the cameras in a fighter by the mechanics; note the collar braiding without collar tabs on the NCO's suit in the foreground.

56. Flowers for a special victory. Note the flying blouse worn over flying trousers and boots, and the variety of uniforms worn by the mechanics and ground crew.

▲52 ▼53

54 ▲ 55 ▼

56 ▼

▲57 ▼58 ▼59

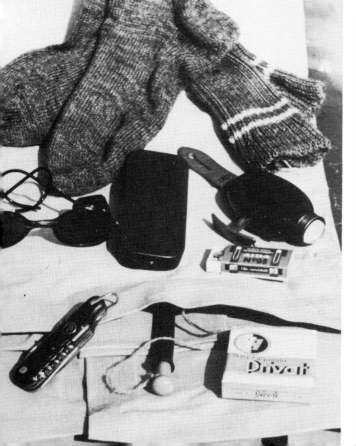

57. Details of early parachute type. Note also the leather flying helmets and large goggles. On the left, just visible, is the collar tab of a specialist with field

officer's rank (Sonderführer) with no wings inside the oakleaves on the collar tab.

58. In the survival bag were also

such items as an inflatable mattress, socks, sunglasses, lamp, etc.

59. The survival bag, with the

seal broken to show the contents.

60. This machete was also one of the most important items of the survival bag.

▲61　▼62　　　　▲63　▼64

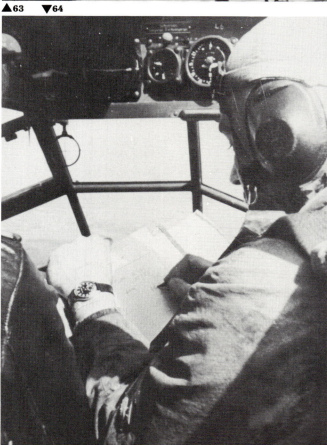

61. Mechanics and their utility and working rigs are far less often portrayed, but their role was vital.

62. Checking the observer's watch with unit's master clock. Note the German Cross in gold worn by the man at right.

63. Preparing to take off on an observation mission. The observer, with document case, boards the aircraft.

64. This observer uses a civilian, not the official model, wristwatch.

65. The pilot. Note the detail of the canvas flying helmet and of the zip on the side of the leg.

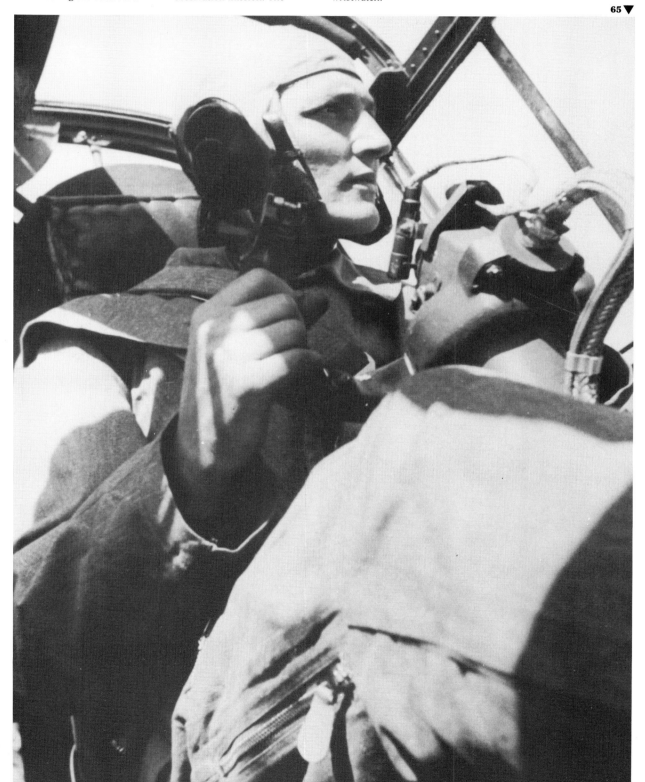

68▲   69▶

66. Machine-gunner in his turret.

67. Return from a mission: note the difference between the pilot's seat parachute and the rear gunner's, who had only a harness with snatch clips to attach the separate parachute bag if needed.

68. The leather flying suit and large goggles. This manually operated camera was used to take indirect pictures with shadows revealing possible targets.

69. This illustration offers a clear view of the system of attaching the oxygen mask to the flying helmet; this is the three-point system, but a two-point system also existed.

▲66   ▼67

▲72

70. Detail of the multi-pocketed 'Channel' trousers; and, in the foreground, detail of the rear part of the inflatable life-jacket.

71. Recruits taking their oath. These men are from the General Goering (later renamed Hermann Goering) Regiment, as indicated by the white collar tabs, the white piping on the other ranks' peaked caps and the special green regimental standards.

72. An early model of the inflatable life-jacket; note also the seat parachute.

▲70 ▼71

73. An interesting picture showing a pre-war quality tunic with branch colour collar piping, down-tailed breast eagle, and an example of a monogram on the shoulder strap; in this case, it denotes a cadre of a training unit, and is embroidered directly into the strap base. (It would have been in white metal for higher NCO ranks and in gilt metal for officers.)

74. Field Marshal Goering before his promotion to the unique rank of Reichsmarschall. He wears a standard tunic and peaked cap (the latter with golden embroidered insignia and golden chinstrap); note especially also his field marshal's baton, Pour le Mérite First World War neck order, the Nazi Blood Order on the right breast, First World War Iron Cross 1st Class, Pilot's Badge and Golden NSDAP Party Badge on left breast.

▲75 ▼76   ▲77

75. A very rare pre-war model of leather flying suit cut on the canvas standard model (note the half yoke on the right shoulder); the other man is a naval officer wearing the Submarine Badge.

76. Three officers from a Luftwaffe field division; note the steel helmet with camouflage cover, the officer's ski cap with silver piping at the crown, the camouflage jackets, the officer's arm rank insignia and the breast eagle being worn.

77. An NCO in Russia wearing one of several models of fur caps.

78. Detail of the officer's side cap with silver piping, compared with the other ranks' side cap (on the left). Note also the end of the tubes of the oxygen masks.

79. Detail of the inflatable life-jacket; note that the Knight's Cross is worn with any uniform order.

78 ▲   79 ▼

80. Good detail of the summer canvas flying suit; the gloves are of civilian origin.

81. A Luftwaffe general (on the left, in leather coat) visits a seaplane unit.

82. This flyer is using a back-parachute rather than a seat one.

83. Before a training flight; note the detail of the helmet, without earphones, the goggles, and the braiding on the corners of the NCO mechanic's collar.

▲80 ▼81

84. Apart from the major giving his orders in the background, all the personnel here are officers and all wear the summer suit.

85. 'Elegance and distinction': note the gloves and the lightweight summer flying helmet.

86. An illustration of the way to strap on the parachute.

87. An excellent view of the canvas flying helmet for summer wear. Note the double buckle/strap system, the hook for the oxygen mask, the leather protection to the earphones, and the unstrapped laryngophone, rarely seen since it was usually hidden by the collar.

The *Fotofax* series

A new range of pictorial studies of military subjects for the modeller, historian and enthusiast. Each title features a carefully-selected set of photographs plus a data section of facts and figures on the topic covered. With line drawings and detailed captioning, every volume represents a succinct and valuable study of the subject. New and forthcoming titles:

Warbirds
F-111 Aardvark
P-47 Thunderbolt
B-52 Stratofortress
Stuka!
Jaguar
US Strategic Air Power: Europe 1942–1945
Dornier Bombers
RAF in Germany

Vintage Aircraft
German Naval Air Service
Sopwith Camel
Fleet Air Arm, 1920–1939
German Bombers of WWI

Soldiers
World War One: 1914
World War One: 1915
World War One: 1916
Union Forces of the American Civil War
Confederate Forces of the American Civil War
Luftwaffe Uniforms
British Battledress 1945–1967 (2 vols)

Warships
Japanese Battleships, 1897–1945
Escort Carriers of World War Two
German Battleships, 1897–1945
Soviet Navy at War, 1941–1945
US Navy in World War Two, 1943–1944
US Navy, 1946–1980 (2 vols)
British Submarines of World War One

Military Vehicles
The Chieftain Tank
Soviet Mechanized Firepower Today
British Armoured Cars since 1945
NATO Armoured Fighting Vehicles
The Road to Berlin
NATO Support Vehicles

The *Illustrated* series

The internationally successful range of photo albums devoted to current, recent and historic topics, compiled by leading authors and representing the best means of obtaining your own photo archive.

Warbirds
US Spyplanes
USAF Today
Strategic Bombers, 1945–1985
Air War over Germany
Mirage
US Naval and Marine Aircraft Today
USAAF in World War Two
B-17 Flying Fortress
Tornado
Junkers Bombers of World War Two
Argentine Air Forces in the Falklands Conflict
F-4 Phantom Vol II
Army Gunships in Vietnam
Soviet Air Power Today
F-105 Thunderchief
Fifty Classic Warbirds
Canberra and B-57
German Jets of World War Two

Vintage Warbirds
The Royal Flying Corps in World War One
German Army Air Service in World War One
RAF between the Wars
The Bristol Fighter
Fokker Fighters of World War One
Air War over Britain, 1914–1918
Nieuport Aircraft of World War One

Tanks
Israeli Tanks and Combat Vehicles
Operation Barbarossa
Afrika Korps
Self-Propelled Howitzers
British Army Combat Vehicles 1945 to the Present
The Churchill Tank
US Mechanized Firepower Today
Hitler's Panzers
Panzer Armee Afrika
US Marine Tanks in World War Two

Warships
The Royal Navy in 1980s
The US Navy Today
NATO Navies of the 1980s
British Destroyers in World War Two
Nuclear Powered Submarines
Soviet Navy Today
British Destroyers in World War One
The World's Aircraft Carriers, 1914–1945
The Russian Convoys, 1941–1945
The US Navy in World War Two
British Submarines in World War Two
British Cruisers in World War One
U-Boats of World War Two
Malta Convoys, 1940–1943

Uniforms
US Special Forces of World War Two
US Special Forces 1945 to the Present
The British Army in Northern Ireland
Israeli Defence Forces, 1948 to the Present
British Special Forces, 1945 to Present
US Army Uniforms Europe, 1944–1945
The French Foreign Legion
Modern American Soldier
Israeli Elite Units
US Airborne Forces of World War Two
The Boer War
The Commandos World War Two to the Present
Victorian Colonial Wars

A catalogue listing these series and other Arms & Armour Press titles is available on request from: Sales Department, Arms & Armour Press, Artillery House, Artillery Row, London SW1P 1RT.